Biblical Principles of Sex

Robert D. Smith, M.D.

TIMELESS TEXTS
Stanley, NC

Contents

Introduction

Believers need to rescue some words of great importance from misuse by the world.[1] One of words is "church." The secular world considers it a necessary evil. Even Christians begin other organizations to do what they think the church should do. The church is a vital part of an instructed believer's life. He knows that it is essential for spiritual growth. Lives are changed through its ministry. It focuses on the needs of all ages, all kinds of people. It is God's plan for ministry outlet. It has a preserving influence in any society.

Some other words needing to be rescued are "virgin birth," "born again," and "baptism." Still other words not found in the Bible but taught by the Bible need rescuing, words like "Trinity" and "sovereignty of God."

One very important word in this latter category is the word "sex." Since God's Word adequately equips believers (II Timothy 3:16, 17) for all of life (II Peter 1:3), the sexual relationship is included. People seek satisfaction in sex but fail to find it because they search outside of marriage and apart from God's principles. Many wrong views of sex have arisen from this search.

Sex is greatly misused and misunderstood by the world. Because unregenerate man lives to satisfy his desires, sex has become exalted as the epitome of human experience. Various techniques are used to increase pleasure in sex. But the new becomes routine, demanding still more new things which also become routine. Biblical guidelines are ignored and violated. Since the goal of the unbeliever's search is personal pleasure (at the cost of biblical principles and personal responsibility),

---

1. This is a revision of an article that originally appeared in *The Journal of Pastoral Practice*, Vol. 7, #2 in 1984. Some of it is based upon the principles given by Jay Adams in *The Christian Counselor's Manual*, pp. 391, 392.

and since such pleasure is so transient and unsatisfying, sex becomes the subject of much caustic humor.

Others have gone to the opposite extreme by attempting to ignore sex. It is almost as though they concluded that since it is so misused, it can't be good. Many, in past generations, thought the physical desire for sex was bad. They grew up in an environment that downgraded or outwardly ignored sex. Some have concluded that the absence of certain words in Scripture means God is silent on the subject. Along with bad hermeneutics, they fall back on human reason and opinion in order to produce their own guidelines for sex.

Some believers, attempting to rescue the word, regrettably have been influenced by views that are as out of balance as the world's. For instance, some attempt to make it the greatest of human marital experiences. One Christian author stated: "God created this one-flesh experience to be the most intense height of physical intimacy and the most profound depth of spiritual oneness between husband and wife."[1] Such a statement implies that if there is a good relationship in sex there will be a good relationship in all other areas of the marriage. Thus a successful sexual life is erroneously made the key to a good marriage. Two other authors say essentially the same thing: a good sexual relationship produces a good marriage.[2]

In their ignorance of biblical teachings, people use terms that equate love and sex. "Make love" and "lovemaking" are a couple of such terms. They thereby distort the meaning of love, especially when they are used to describe sex outside of marriage. These terms also communicate that love is mainly seen in sex and that sex is the most important part of love and marriage. One author calls sex "The Act of Marriage"[3] and repeatedly refers to the sex act as lovemaking. The title erro-

---

1. H. J. Miles, *Sexual Happiness in Marriage*, Zondervan, Grand Rapids, 1967, p. 27.
2. T. LaHaye, B. LaHaye, *The Act of Marriage*, Zondervan, Grand Rapids, 1976.
3. *Ibid.*

neously communicates that sex is *the* act of marriage. All this equates love and sex and ignores other acts of marriage and love which have nothing to do with sex.

Others have attempted to ignore sex. Some speak as if sex is not something good from God. They don't teach about sex in the home and refuse to allow it to be taught in the church. This was vividly illustrated to me many years ago by a fellow deacon. The pastor and deacons of the church we were members of at that time were discussing the possibility of my wife and I teaching some of the biblical principles of sex to young people. This older Christian brother (who loved the Lord, was a treasured friend of mine, and is now with the Lord) replied: "We can talk about anything in the church, but not that!" In spite of his love for the Lord, he ignored all that the Scriptures say on the subject and gave the impression that God has no guidelines for sexual relationships or answers to sexual problems.

Some think it is not necessary to teach about sex to a couple planning on marriage because the husband automatically knows all that he needs to know. The fact is, this is far from the truth. Biblical principles of sex are rarely, if at all, taught in the home or the church. Such an attitude ignores God's plan for sexual relations in marriage found in the Scriptures. It also gives the impression that God is silent, that He has no guidelines for sexual relationships and has no answers for sexual problems.

These erroneous views have produced many problems. The results for Christians can be devastating. Believers may become involved with sex outside marriage. They may deal with their problems no better than non-believers do. Promises of victory seem to have no reality. God and His Word appear to have no answers. The one going outside of marriage for sex is guilty of sin. But the one left may also be guilty of violating other biblical principles, making it easy, though never justifiable, for the spouse to look for satisfaction outside of marriage.

In many marriages, the husband and wife are unhappy and in conflict over sex. They correctly refuse to go outside marriage for satisfaction but live unhappily with unsolved sexual conflicts. Their attempts to ignore them are unsuccessful. Attempts to solve conflicts produce no solutions but only arguments. In those homes, the children have little expectations of success in their own marriages. They see problems, have questions, but get no answers.

All this is happening in *Christian* homes, in the homes of faithful church members, church leaders – even pastors and missionaries. Yet it is all so unnecessary because God's Word has vital principles to guide believers into God-honoring, satisfying sexual relationships.

Believers need to aggressively rescue the word "sex" from all such misuse. They must refuse to follow the world's philosophy in thinking and actions. The Church of Jesus Christ alone has truth. The wolves have come, and believers cannot remain silent hirelings! Believers must apply vital teachings of the Word of God to their own lives to prevent problems in all areas of life. When problems occur, these same biblical principles provide answers.

This book presents six biblical principles fundamental to all sex between married believers. All counselors should be familiar with them. This is not all the Bible says about sex, but these principles are foundational to a satisfying, happy sexual relationship in marriage.

1

Pure and Holy

Sex in marriage is pure and holy; Genesis 1:31.

This first principle is found in the Genesis 1 account of God's creation. On the sixth day, He made human life and created Adam and Eve as sexual beings. Their differences were based on their gender, their sexuality, their being male and female (verse 27). They were not male or female because of sex organs. It is almost as though God made male or female and gave each the appropriate sex organs.[1] God made them the gender they are, and the genitalia identify what God did. God Himself instructed them to engage in sexual relations (verse 28).

It is important to note God's view of His creative actions (including sex) on the sixth day in verse 31:

> Then God saw everything that He had made, and indeed it was very good. So the evening and the morning were the sixth day. (NKJV)

All He made was good, very good. God's view of sex, therefore, is that it is very good. While sex in marriage was not designed as the outlet for the passions of sinful man, sexual desire, unperverted, is a pure, good, holy gift for man to use to glorify God. Sexuality came into being *before* the fall and *before* sin.

But even after sin and the fall of man, God still called marriage good and honorable.

> Marriage must be honored by everybody, and the marriage bed must be unpolluted; God will

---

1. This is important when dealing with such issues as hysterectomy or mastectomy. Loss of the sexual organs does not alter the gender or sexuality since that was created by God.

judge immoral people and adulterers. (Hebrews 13:4 CCNT)

The word for marriage bed in that verse is *koite* (in Greek, "bed"), similar to our English word coitus, which means sexual intercourse. The verse might be translated, "Coitus in marriage is honorable and undefiled." God calls sex in marriage good, honorable, pure, holy, undefiled because He made it that way. Any other view is sinful and unbiblical. Wrong uses of sex are not bad because sex is bad but because people violate biblical principles.

Years ago I was counseling a young married women who had many problems in her life. Even though she was married and had children, one of those problems stemmed from sexual activity with her husband. In the school she attended in childhood she was told, "Nice girls don't *do* that." She was never told that nice girls *do* do that in marriage. She heard her mother complain, "That's all a man wants." Her parents slept in separate bedrooms. Her father complained that his wife wouldn't sleep with him. Now this young woman had serious problems in her sexual relationship. She didn't even like to talk about it. When asked about the problems with this part of her life all she could say was, "It's, it's yukky." It was important for her to see that her view was completely opposite to God's view. She was placing a label on something God created not awful, distasteful, and disagreeable, but "good."

Those who call sex dirty or "yukky" have a sinful view of sex. Those who are uncomfortable and embarrassed talking about or dealing with sex have learned a sinful view of sex. It is certainly not God's view. Unless this view is altered, they too may teach that attitude to their children by their words and actions. When a husband gives his wife a love pat on the buttocks and she responds with a glare and a sharp "Stop that!" she is giving some very poor sex education to her children. Admittedly, he should be discreet, but not prudish. God's attitude toward sex helps provide a good environment for sex education and pre-marital counseling in the home.

Sexual relations in marriage are just as pure and holy as praying, reading the Bible, preparing a message, preaching, tithing, witnessing to someone about his soul, or teaching a Sunday School class. Any lesser view is sinful. Remember, God Himself calls the sexual relationship good, pure, and honorable. Since obedience to God is an act of worship, speaking about sex as God does and obeying God's guidelines for sex might be called an act of worship. When I teach on the subject I treat it with reverence and do not deal with it lightly with a lot of jokes.

One more important fact about God's creation of sexual relationships needs to be added: God reserved sex for marriage; the *only* place it is pure and holy is in marriage. He designed it in such a way that the ultimate delights can be experienced only in marriage. People can experience the physical sensations of the relationship without marriage, of course. But that is no more significant that eating a piece of pie. There may be pleasant physical sensations but, frankly, they have less benefit than the pie! The real delights of sex require the commitment and intimacy only found in the covenant of marriage.

The world's wrong standards for the use of sex must not be the Christian's measure of what is good or bad. The world has stolen sex and thinks the delights are available without marriage. They say this is where you find excitement and real living. But the Bible teaches that the exact opposite is true. One cannot violate God's principles of sex and avoid consequences. Consenting adults do not make fornication or adultery right by consenting. According to the Bible, God will personally deal with their sin; Hebrews 13:4 teaches that "God will judge immoral people and adulterers" (CCNT). In 1 Thessalonians 4:6 we read that "the Lord is the avenger of all such, as we also forewarned you and testified" (NKJV).

Any persons who refuse to see sex in marriage as pure, holy, and good and honorable need biblical counseling.

2

The Nature of Physical Union

Sex is not the basis for marriage, and marriage is not first and foremost a physical union; John 4:16–18.

Some have erroneously taken the position that marriage is not consummated until sex has occurred.[1] This allows dissolution of a marriage when there has been no sexual relations, since, according to this view, a marriage has not yet occurred. One author states, "The wedding ceremony in itself is not the act that really unites a couple in holy matrimony in the eyes of God; it merely grants them the public license to retreat privately to some romantic spot and experience the 'one-flesh' relationship that truly unites them as husband and wife."[2] Some even misuse the Old Testament account of Isaac and Rebecca to teach that until marriage is "consummated" by sex they are not considered married. But this is not a biblical teaching.

Christ's position on this was different. We see this in His discussion with the woman at the well in John 4:16–18

> Jesus said to her, "Go, call your husband, and come here." The woman answered and said, "I have no husband." Jesus said to her, "You have well said, 'I have no husband,' for you have had five husbands, and the one whom you now have is not your husband; in that you spoke truly." (NKJV)

She previously had five husbands. In contrast, He told her the man she was living with at that time was not her husband. Having sexual relations with him did not constitute marriage.

---

1. Murray J, *Divorce*, Presbyterian and Reformed, Philadelphia, 1961, p. 38.
2. LaHaye, op. cit., p. 12.

Sexual intercourse, legal or illicit, does not produce or break a marriage in God's eyes. Sexual intercourse, then, is not the basis for marriage. Throughout the Scriptures marriage is considered a *covenantal* relationship begun by a public legal ceremony where a couple enters into the covenant with one another. A couple is just as married after being pronounced husband and wife as they are after their first sexual intercourse after the ceremony. And though adultery seriously hurts a marriage, the marriage persists – unless broken by death or divorce.

Although marriage is not simply legalized sex, and sex is not the basis of marriage, sex is very important. It is a very prominent and essential part of marriage. Failure of either person to participate in sexual relations wholeheartedly, aggressively, and passionately is sin and ought to be called "sin." We preach and teach faithfully about hell, the cross, the blood, and the resurrection. We ought to teach and preach just as faithfully that not to participate in sex in marriage wholeheartedly, aggressively, and passionately is sin. It is disobeying God. It is dishonoring Christ. It is sinning against your mate.

I am amazed by married people professing to be believers, claiming to be right with Jesus Christ, sitting in the pews of Bible-believing churches who disobey God, dishonor Christ, and sin against their mates by being very passive about sex. Passiveness about sex is no more biblical than passiveness about prayer, Bible study, tithing, or church attendance. Passive sex in marriage is unbiblical, selfish sex. By such inaction passive marriage partners indicate that God's Word and their mates are not important enough to put forth the effort. It's amazing how many believers say they want to grow but ignore growth in this area. They say they want to obey God's Word then volitionally choose to treat sex their own way. This sort of sinfulness is appalling. We get upset when people obey God halfheartedly in other areas, and should in this one also. God called the sexual relationship "very good." He commanded Adam and Eve to enter into the relationship. Since it is so important, every Christian husband and every Christian wife must be enthusiastically involved in the riches of a biblical sexual relationship.

Even so, sex is not the basis for marriage or the most important part of marriage. Marriage is not first and foremost a physical union. Although marriage does legalize sex, the physical relationship is not first and foremost; it is not what makes a marriage successful. There is far more to unity in marriage than sex. Before sexual unity there must be a spiritual and mental unity that provides genuine companionship.

3

Giving is the Goal

The primary goal of sexual relationship is giving sexual satisfaction to your spouse; 1 Corinthians 7.

This principle is taught in 1 Corinthians 7. The context of this passage (1 Corinthians 6:15–7:9) is sex in marriage. In chapter six, Paul has been describing some of the basic aspects of marital sex. He has noted the oneness that occurs sexually.[1] He has also mentioned the misuse of the sexual relationship outside of marriage. Then, in chapter seven Paul suggests some ways to avoid fornication and then discusses the sexual relationship in marriage.

Many times, when God talks to parents, he uses generic terms such as "parent" (or at times "father") to refer to both father and mother. In this verse (and the next), doubtless, to make certain there is no misunderstanding, the Holy Spirit inspired Paul to speak to each spouse specifically rather than in generic terms. The Spirit wants both husband and wife to realize that each has a responsibility in the matter of sexual relationships. He says the same thing to both but makes certain that it is said to each individually. He first speaks to the husband, then to the wife; exactly what He says to one He says to the other. Both have equal responsibility in their sexual relationship. Note, too, that here God gave a command, not an encouragement. The same command is given to both husband and wife. This is not something that one spouse or the other can decide to take or leave.

Let us now look at what He says in 1 Corinthians 7:3.

---

1. In comparing the sexual oneness to our unity with the Lord I have often questioned if He is saying that the delights of the sexual relationship in some measure mirror the delight and satisfaction of our oneness with Jesus Christ.

> Let the husband render to his wife the affection due her, and likewise also the wife to her husband. (NKJV)

> The husband must fulfill his obligation to his wife and the wife also must do the same for her husband. (CCNT)

The word "affection" is "benevolence" in the King James translation and can be translated "good." In the context of the passage this refers to the good that results from the sexual relationship. They are married, and she is to receive something good from her husband. He is to do her good, which means he is to satisfy her sexual desires. The word "due" implies an obligation she is to receive from her husband. This means something he is required to supply. Other translations (such as the CCNT) speak of this as an obligation the husband must fulfill. Because it is due her, it is his responsibility and obligation to provide this good, which is the satisfaction of her sexual desires. Not only is it due, but the Spirit emphasizes the fact by prefacing the command with "let...render" or "must fulfill." In a sense, there is a double command.

The husband is required to render or fulfill, which means to give fully, completely, without reluctance, hesitation, or inhibition. He is required to fulfill the sexual needs and desires of his mate enthusiastically and joyfully. Thus Paul is saying the primary goal of the sexual relationship is meeting the sexual needs of one's spouse. To make certain that wives do not misunderstand, the Spirit inspired Paul to say the same thing to them: "Likewise also the wife unto the husband." The wife has the same obligation and responsibility to satisfy her husband's sexual desires and needs completely, enthusiastically, and without reluctance. Each is given the responsibility of keeping the other sexually satisfied.

When God created human beings with the desire for sexual activity and commanded them to use their bodies sexually, He also designed the delights to be only found in marriage. As stated previously, the sexual relationship is not simply limited to and permitted in marriage but God mandates it and makes it an obligation. Obedience to this command prevents and makes useless the futile attempts to satisfy this desire with anyone other than one's spouse.

Love seeks to give in order to satisfy another. Scripture shows that the primary definition of the word love is "giving." John 3:16 says that "God so loved the world that He *gave* His only Son." Galatians 2:20 tells that Christ "loved me and *gave* Himself up for me." Ephesians 5:25 says that "Christ loved the church and *gave* Himself up for her." The focus of love is on giving to others. In fact, according to Acts 20:35, Jesus taught that the greater pleasure that we receive is through giving: "It is more blessed to give than to receive" (CCNT). If love is the basis for sex, the goal of the sexual relationship is giving, not getting.

Books that teach giving-to-get try to motivate a giving attitude, but it is through a selfish motive: husbands are instructed to do loving deeds for their wives so that they will be more responsive and thus will return more love with more enthusiasm. Of course, if the husband gives in order to get pleasure, his goal is still wrong because he has made pleasure his goal. Doing the right thing with the wrong motive does not make the thing right. Also to focus on *getting* is an evidence of lust and selfishness; lust seeks its own satisfaction. Giving to get is selfish and violates the principle of 2 Corinthians 5:15 which teaches that believers should no longer live selfishly for themselves as they once did when nonbelievers. When one seeks to get pleasure through the sexual relationship, that pleasure will be less satisfying and less intense than the pleasure that is the by-product of giving according to biblical principles. Husbands (and wives) are to continue doing loving deeds with the biblical motive of pleasing God and their spouses. They are to be more excited and joyful about this than about satisfying themselves.

All this is not to say that pleasure and climax are bad. God designed these as a part of the sexual relationship and, therefore, they cannot be called bad. Climax is not wrong but it cannot be the guiding principle or the goal. It is the natural by-product of pleasing your spouse. Satisfying your spouse may or may not include climax. Your spouse is the one who decides. One should not receive personal satisfaction in the sexual relationship, nor achieve climax, unless he is intensely satisfied by knowing that he has used his body to provide sexual satisfaction for his mate. The key principle of all sexual relationships is the same principle God's Word teaches for all of life: true satisfaction is not based on what we get from life, but is based on how we please God and obey Him.

Many people do not understand this principle. A husband may try to manipulate his wife *to* sex. He may attempt this with pornography or simply demand that she satisfy him. A wife may try to manipulate her husband *with* sex. It is a reward for pleasing her. They need to change their thinking and actions to conform to the biblical principle.

At times wives complain, "The only time my husband shows affection is when he wants sex." He is only warm, loving, and gentle when he wants something. If he shows her affection only when he wants sex, his affection has a selfish, self-centered motive. His giving to get is very obvious to her. The biblical principle is that he is to be affectionate because he desires to show love and warmth to his wife, not because of any ulterior motives. At all times a husband must show his wife the same warmth of the deepest affection that he shows when he is sexually aroused.

There will be times when it is important for the husband to stop short of sexual activity. He must show his wife that he loves her by action and words in spite of the fact that sexual intercourse does not occur. When he sees that his wife is not responding, he should let her know of his love for her and his willingness to go to sleep if she wishes (but he must see to it that he doesn't leave her aroused and unsatisfied). This is difficult when the desire for intercourse is very strong, but if his goal is to satisfy his wife and show her that he loves her under all circumstances, it will be easier. He must not become bitter through self-centered resentment that he hasn't been satisfied.

He may argue, "But that is not my nature!" That is very true, but your nature is not to guide your sexual relationship. "Natural" means being comfortable with sinful habits. God wants believers to quit being natural and become more and more like Christ (Who is the standard for what is normal). The husband is to live by God's Word rather than his nature. The Bible tells how to be pleasing to Him even when it is not natural to do so.

Some husbands think that the only thing that satisfies his wife is for her to have a climax. They are able to achieve a very pleasant climax with every intercourse, so they believe that for her to enjoy intercourse she also must experience one. For some men, her involvement in the sexual activity is heightened by achieving climax, so he attempts to reach that point *for his own benefit*. This can be very exhausting when she does not desire to have a climax. They may work and work and work in an unsuccessful attempt to produce a climax, which may cause her frustration or even dislike of the sexual relationship. A wife may be satisfied with intercourse without climax for herself, because it provides a closeness with her husband and provides an opportunity to satisfy him. She may enjoy the warmth, affection, closeness, and intimacy that goes along with intercourse to his climax. It is not wrong for a husband to have intercourse and climax without his wife having climax so long as he is seeking to please her and meet her needs. This means focusing on her interests and desires as more important than his own. She is the one to decide. He is to satisfy her by her guidelines, not his ideas.

Too frequently, a husband has incorrectly used this principle to demand that his wife satisfy his desire. When he demands that she obey God he is taking God's job away from God. Only God can demand obedience to His command. The husband does not have that authority. In addition, when he becomes demanding, he tempts her to demand that he satisfy her desires. The result is two self-centered, selfish people demanding to have what they want. This is not love.

Admittedly a number of problems must be solved to follow this Scriptural guideline. A husband needs an erection in order to function sexually. Our society teaches, by design and default, that the husband's erection occurs from his anticipation of the pleasure he will receive. Thus the focus is on what he will get out of the relationship. This is not biblical. From I Corinthians 7:3 it can be inferred that an erection should occur in anticipation of meeting the needs of his wife and giving her pleasure. The erection should occur not primarily for his own pleasure but to be prepared to give pleasure.

Another problem is that the erection cannot be achieved by a direct act of the will. It is achieved through some mental or physical stimulation. The natural result of the erection is the desire for intercourse and further pleasure. As a result of the curse of sin, even the normal physiologic process becomes self-centered. When a husband develops sexual desires and habits by wrong principles he will use sex for self-satisfaction. Thus he will need to change to meet the biblical goal of finding his greatest pleasure in giving, not in receiving. Along with this he will need to change his focus on his own feeling to a focus on his wife's. He must retrain himself to experience sexual preparedness through the delight of giving and pleasing his wife. The satisfaction that comes from pleasing God and his wife is to be his primary goal.

It is proper, at this point, to discuss the terms "needs" and "desires." Our culture uses the word "needs" in a manner that focuses on getting those needs supplied. The philosophy is that if your needs are not met, you will suffer damage of some kind. In most cases these needs are something that are to be supplied by someone else. But what are "needs?" The word "need" does imply something without which the individual will suffer harm. It refers to the body's need for food, water, rest, and so on. Failure to supply those needs will result in harm to the body. A responsible steward takes care of the body by supplying food, water, and rest in sufficient quality and quantity. In a believer's life, if these bodily needs are not met, there may be temporary physical discomfort and even permanent physical damage, but neither prevents the believer from obeying God. If this continues, the body will ultimately die and the believer will enter Heaven. There may be physical damage to the body, but it results in the believer's gain. I say this not to encourage neglect of the body, because the believer is responsible to take care of his body as the temple of the Holy Spirit. If, however, through no fault of his own, physical needs are not met and damage does occur, there is no eternal damage. If we think of needs as something that *must* be supplied to the individual, without which the person will experience irreparable eternal damage, actually there is only *one* human need: the need of a Savior.

Sexual "needs" can be treated as physical needs. There will be no eternal damage if they are not supplied. In fact, in contrast to physical needs, failure to supply this need will not produce any physical harm to the one deprived. So what are "sexual needs"? Actually, there are none. But it may help in a marriage relationship to think of the matter this way: Look at your spouse's desires as needs you are required to satisfy. Inaction on your past will not prevent damage to your spouse since none will occur. The main issue is whether you are pleasing God by satisfying your spouse's desires. As a matter of fact, to treat your spouse's desires as needs (which you are required to supply) aids your spiritual growth and prevents spiritual damage to you rather than your spouse. Thus the only time you can use the term "sexual needs" is in relation to your spouse. You cannot focus on your needs (since there are none) and insist that your spouse satisfy them. Using this definition, these "needs" of yours are actually desires and no harm will come to you if they are not supplied.[1]

An essential part of the sexual relationship is loving, open, biblical *communication*. This will contribute to answer-

---

1. Those who claim that unsatisfied sexual needs will produce emotional problems are using secular philosophies to manipulate satisfaction of per-

ing the appropriate question, "How do I know what pleases my mate?" In order to know what pleases each other the husband and wife should each make a list of all the things the other person can do that provide pleasure and satisfaction in the sexual relationship. This list should be as detailed as possible. Then each is to give the list to the other and give up the right to everything that is on his own original list. You may ask, "If I tell my spouse what pleases me, isn't that focusing on myself?" This depends on how you respond to what your spouse does with that information.

This might be illustrated as follows: Husband, before you leave for work, suppose your wife asks you what you want for dinner. After a moment of thought you tell her you would like steak. Are you being selfish? We don't know yet. Your request for steak either was made to help her fulfill her responsibility to be the kind of wife, mother, and housekeeper she should be or was done as a dictator. You go off to work anticipating a succulent steak dinner when you get home. However when you sit down to dinner after work with your mouth watering for it, there is no steak. Instead, your wife has fixed a "wonder casserole" (you wonder what's in it). Your response when you see that casserole will show your motive for sharing the information with her. If you become angry and react sinfully, by blowing up or clamming up, your request was not to help her. It was not honest communication but a selfish demand.

However if, after you take a bite of the casserole, with a twinkle in your eye (not as sarcasm) you say something like this to her, "This is delicious. I've never had steak that tasted like this before! How did you get it to have such an unusual flavor?" you are pleasing God by your response. Thus your original request was simple honest communication without

---

sonal desires. The only problem one actually has if he does not get what he wants is unsatisfied physical desire (which is not an emotional problem). That which is really a part of self-discipline and which is repeatedly taught by the Scripture as a part of spiritual growth cannot be harmful.

any demand. If you tell your wife how much you enjoy the food and appreciate her efficient use of leftovers, your original request was not selfish. You are giving her information she requested and could use.

The same is true in the sexual relationship. When the husband communicates his desire for satisfaction and his wife responds in a negative way, the goal for his communication will be measured by his response. If he is angry and unloving because she fails to satisfy him, he actually demanded satisfaction selfishly. If, by contrast, he gives her warm, loving affection, expresses his love to her, thanks God for her, and goes to sleep, he was communicating in a biblical way. He honestly stated his desire and he is not angry because she failed to satisfy that desire.

As stated above, an aid in biblical communication in making the lists is giving up the right to everything on the list. This means that neither can expect nor demand one single item on the list. To repeat, demanding is selfishness and violates the biblical principles being discussed. Reacting to failure with coldness, unkindness, harshness, or criticism is sinful selfishness. When each person makes the list and gives it to his spouse and doesn't receive any of the items on that list, he must still focus on pleasing his spouse, thanking God for that spouse, and meeting the spouse's desires, and not on the fact that he's not getting anything on the list. This is what makes giving up the right to have anything on the list so important. I Corinthians 10:13 promises victory even in this circumstance. God knows that a husband in this situation is able to handle life without "steak." Open, honest communication of desires must not be the only topic of communication, nor must it be used to manipulate the other.

As a part of their communication, the husband and wife also need to discuss what may hinder the satisfaction of the sexual desire at a given moment. Again, this must be done very carefully with the attitude of aiding, not of trying to manipulate the other to get what one wants. Again, the goal is to satisfy one's spouse.

The husband needs to use these concepts at times when he is very sexually aroused but his wife does not seem to have any interest. All I said above does not prohibit his honest communication of a desire for intercourse. His wife may participate with him for the purpose of satisfying him, and he may be the only one to achieve climax. This is not wrong, but he cannot make self-satisfaction the dominant part of their sexual relationship. If, when he expresses his desire, she refuses, then he must follow the above principles and show love and affection without going on to intercourse. This is difficult when the desire is strong but the grace of God will enable him to do the loving thing, which is to please God by pleasing his spouse. If she refuses, what pleases her at that time is no sexual activity. Being godly at such a time requires the grace of God and is evidence of godly manhood. When a man demands satisfaction of his desires he is like a child and not manly. Manliness is being like Christ, not like a child.

To review, the primary goal of the sexual relationship is meeting the desires of one's spouse. The primary focus of the sexual relationship is *giving*, not *getting*, pleasure. Any pleasure that's received must be secondary to the primary goal of giving pleasure. Pleasure is not wrong, but it must not be the goal or the motive, but the by-product of giving pleasure to the spouse.

This principle, that the goal of the sexual relationship is to provide satisfaction for a person's spouse, helps with a number of other sexually related issues.

For one thing, a couple should plan their marriage in such a way that the satisfying of sexual desires is not hindered by contraceptive methods. The satisfying of the sexual relationship should not be built around its reproductive aspects. One example is the rhythm method, which restricts satisfying one another to times when conception is not likely. When the wife is fertile (unless they desire a child), unrestricted satisfying of either one's desires is impossible. In the rhythm system the couple can only obey God's command when their plans make it possible. They should find a method of contraception that allows for satisfaction of the sexual desires at any time.

This principle opposes any other method of satisfying sexual desires. Thus it opposes masturbation. The goal of masturbation is satisfying self, not a spouse; it is getting rather than giving. Masturbation is selfishly satisfying one-self sexually. In the fantasies that are a part of masturbation, other people are controlled for personal benefit. Masturbation develops sexual thoughts and actions that are motivated by self-gratification. Those thoughts and actions become selfish habits that produce difficulties in marriage. People try to approve masturbation by saying the sexual desire is like thirst and hunger. This is an invalid comparison. Satisfying the sexual desire, unlike hunger, is not essential to the welfare of the physical body. Failure to satisfy hunger or thirst can harm the body. In contrast, failure to satisfy sexual desire produces no physical harm. In the past, some have concluded that mastur-bation was harmful to the body and would cause some kind of mental or physical problems. Many, as an excuse to justify masturbation, have pointed to the incorrectness of that con-cept. Admittedly, it is true that masturbation does not do any physical harm to the body.[1] But without any proof, they have gone to the other extreme and erroneously claim that not sat-isfying the desire will cause emotional and physical harm. Satisfying hunger is essential to responsible care of the tem-ple of the Holy Spirit; the focus of sexual activity is to satisfy the desire of one's spouse, not self.[2] Because the person who masturbates focuses on satisfying self and builds those kinds of selfish habits, when he marries he will have considerable

---

1. Regrettably, even some believers have attempted to justify masturbation with that logic.
2. Some argue that the primary reason for sexual activity is reproduction. In fact, they argue that harm will come if the desire is not satisfied in that reproduction will not occur and the race will die out. However, that is not what this passage in 1 Corinthians teaches. Reproduction is a by-product of satisfying one's spouse. There is still no resulting physical harm to a person from not satisfying the sexual desire.

difficulty changing the focus from getting satisfaction to giving it. The marriage ceremony does not automatically break habits of masturbation and the fantasies that accompany it. When sexual activity does not occur with the frequency of that person's desire, the person who has not had victory over masturbation before marriage will probably resort to that selfish view of sex.

The focus on giving, not getting, pleasure also deals with the issue of so-called adult movies and pornography. This whole industry is far from "adult." Consider what motivates a child. The central focus for a child, that which motivates his actions, is getting what he wants; when he does not, he attempts to manipulate others by making life miserable for them until he gets what he wants. In 1 Corinthians 13, Paul says one of the manifestations of an adult is the putting off of childish things. This means an adult changes his focus from getting what he wants to giving for the benefit of others. Not only is this the difference between an adult and a child but Paul says this is the difference between a believer and a non-believer. "And He died for all, that those who live should live no longer for themselves, but for Him who died for them and rose again" (2 Corinthians 5:15, NKJV). The non-believer still functions as a child seeking what he wants in life. In contrast, the believer does not seek to satisfy himself in life but seeks to please God, who redeemed him from slavery to sin, selfishness, and self-satisfaction.

Since the pornographic industry focuses on selfishness, self-satisfaction, and getting pleasure, this means that adult movies are anything but adult. Other people are used for selfish purposes. Also, pornography is a lie, promising a wonderful, delightful experience – that is only fantasy. Because it is so selfish it certainly is not adult! Also much of the so-called sophisticated humor and adult movies on television and in the theatre today are built on anything but adult concepts. They are not sophisticated or adult, but immature and childish.

On this subject, it is also important to mention the subject of so-called "sexual addiction." The problem a sex addict has is not with an addiction but with worship. He is worshipping sexual pleasure over pleasing God. It has become a habit he would rather not break. Sinful desires can never be satisfied. The person who uses the addiction label to justify the use of pornography is actually attempting to satisfy an insatiable, enslaving, habitual desire. The only source of any real satisfaction is through a right relationship with God.

This goal of giving, not getting, also opposes homosexuality. In addition to the numerous prohibitions of homosexuality in the Bible, the biblical principles of sex oppose it. The Bible teaches that sex is reserved for a man and a woman who are husband and wife – whose goal is to please one another, not themselves.

Different forms of human reasoning have been used to portray homosexuality as normal and desirable. In one of her columns, Ann Landers tried to encourage some parents who were distressed about their son's homosexual behavior by saying science has proven their son was born that way. Scientific claims have been made in support of her statement, but the alleged evidence fails the scientific standards of proof. We have benefited greatly from the improvements science has produced. But science is just as fallible as any other human activity. Science cannot set the standard for normal conduct. Many absolute conclusions by science have been absolutely incorrect. People were observed sailing out on the ocean and never coming back. This was an objective empirical piece of data from which the observers concluded the earth was flat. Later the sun was observed coming up in the east and setting in the west. This happened daily for years and also was an objective empirical piece of data. So they concluded the sun revolved around the earth. This latter view even became a part of the theology of the Catholic church. The scientists taught it, so the theologians made it a part of their theology. Then when another scientist came along with a new instrument called the telescope with which he did some objective measuring, his results were considered heresy because they disagreed with the church's stand. Science is not infallible, and has not proven that homosexuality is normal for anyone.

With the primary goal of the sexual relationship being directed toward a spouse, this increases the responsibility for parents to provide biblical sex education in the home. Children need to learn that their bodies do not exist for their own benefit. When a little child plays with his or her sexual organ, the child needs to be taught that that was not given for the child to play with, but for special purposes designed by God. They can observe one function, which is the elimination of bodily waste. If a child asks for further information the question can be answered by saying God has reserved another function for use after marriage. As the child grows older and asks for more details, these can be given. But the emphasis of the teaching ought to be that the motive for that function is to please God and a future spouse. This helps the child grow up understanding and accepting God's principle that the primary goal for the use of the body is not for self-centered purposes. Once more, this emphasis provides a superior answer to the heavy influence of our culture, which focuses on getting.

Since the only right way to satisfy sexual desire is through satisfying a spouse, stimulating one to arouse sexual desire is automatically reserved for marriage. This brings us to the subject of premarital sex. Petting is sexual stimulation outside of marriage and is stimulating sexual desires that cannot be righteously satisfied. A specialist in diseases of the kidneys, bladder, and male sexual organs (urologist) made this statement to me: "A kiss is the first step of intercourse." This man was not trying to promote morality, just describing normal human physiology. Stimulation of sexual desire in each other by a husband and wife is very proper and is called "foreplay." Young people who think they can pet and stop short of intercourse miss the delights of pleasing God and each other sexually and are building habits that will plague them in the future. They are building sex on a selfish relationship that will carry over into their marriage. Once those habits are developed, marriage does not automatically correct them.

They can be changed biblically with God's help but that is more difficult than preventing them. The best solution is prevention by building biblical habits of thinking and action before marriage.

A young man may attempt to manipulate his girlfriend or fiancé into sexual activity by telling her that he loves her and if she loves him she will use sex as an expression of her love for him. So in order to keep him and the relationship, she gives in and they start sexual activity. Once they are married this premarital activity will reap an agonizing harvest. She begins to realize she no longer needs to give in to him to keep him and becomes more and more involved in the responsibilities of being a good housekeeper and mother. Along with this she becomes less involved and less interested in sex. But she also sees that the only time he seems to pay any attention to her is for the sexual relationship. She becomes offended, believing she is only valuable to him as a sex partner, and her enthusiasm wanes even further. He can't understand what is happening. Before marriage she was very willing and eager to participate. Now the frequency is declining. He gets upset and expresses this to her. This kind of communication only increases her belief that his main interest in her is for sex. This cools off her interest even more, which causes him more frustration, and so the cycle goes. They are both reaping the harvest of their selfishness in premarital sex. Both of them selfishly used the other for personal gain; he used her for sexual pleasure, she used him for companionship benefits. Those selfish habits need to be replaced by the biblical principles presented in this book. If they have so sinned, they must repent and use these principles to help them rebuild their relationship biblically. This is also true if a pregnancy results from their premarital action.

4

Equally Able

God has created both husband and wife with equal
ability to satisfy each other; 1 Corinthians 7:4.

The wife does not have authority over her own body, but the husband does. And likewise the husband does not have authority over his own body, but the wife does (NKJV).

The wife doesn't have authority over her own body; rather it is her husband who does. Also, the husband doesn't have authority over his own body; rather it is his wife who does (CCNT).

The wife does not have authority over her own body, but the husband does; and likewise also the husband does not have authority over his own body, but the wife does (NASB).

Following the principle of verse three, the word "authority" ("power" in KJV) means the wife does not have the authority to use her body as the standard for the success of their sexual relationship. Satisfaction of her desires is not the standard for her. The way she determines the proper use of her body is when her husband's desires are satisfied. The standard for the right use of her body rests in her husband. Her body is to be used for her husband's benefit, which is to satisfy his sexual desires. As we have seen, her guideline in the sexual relationship is her husband's satisfaction.

Then the command is repeated to the husband. Even though it is redundant, it is important to repeat to the husband the identical statements as above. Following the principle of verse three, the word "authority" means the husband does not have the right to use his body as the standard for the success of their sexual relationship. Satisfaction of his desires

29

is not the standard for him. The way he determines the proper use of his body is when his wife's desires are satisfied. The standard for the right use of his body rests in his wife. His body is to be used for his wife's benefit, which is to satisfy her sexual desires. His guideline in the sexual relationship is his wife's satisfaction.

Again God gives the identical command to both the husband and the wife. Since God gave each the same command, then, in God's eyes, each has equal ability to obey. He would not give them the same command and make their ability or desire different. There are differences in anatomy and physiology, but these are complimentary. One is not greater or more important than the other. Since God gave them equal ability He is saying to both husband and wife, "You are commanded to use your body to provide complete sexual satisfaction for your mate, and you have the ability to obey. Your ability does not exist for your own pleasure but to please your spouse." God's command is to focus on what is given not on what is received. This principle removes the right of either one to demand or expect satisfaction from the other. The standard is spouse satisfaction, not self-satisfaction.

This equal authority and ability solves a long-standing misconception. For years we have been taught that the husband is the aggressor, or initiator, and the wife the responder. The wife has been taught that she is not to participate in the sexual relationship until her husband initiates it. This teaching treats her as a sex object for her husband, while her desires are to be ignored or minimized. The implication is that a wife who is aggressive in the sexual relationship is violating God's principles. Yet God's Word in this passage contradicts such ideas. People have tried to determine response on the basis of their own observations rather than on God's Word. Some secular people using unbiblical principles in research[1] have concluded from that research the same thing the Scrip-

---

1. Masters W. M., Johnson V. E., *Human Sexual Response*, Little, Brown, Boston, 1966; *Human Sexual Inadequacies*, Little, Brown, Boston, 1970.

ture is teaching: husband and wife possess equal ability in the sexual area. Because of the research, people are beginning to give up some of the erroneous ideas of the past. It is regrettable that believers take a biblical position only after non-believers agree with the biblical position through unbiblical methods.

It is interesting that in verse 3 Paul first spoke to the husband. In verse 4 he speaks to the wife first. Although the specific reason is not given, at least the Holy Spirit is emphasizing the importance of the wife being a leader in the sexual relationship. She is not to wait passively for her husband but she also is to initiate sexual activity.

Some wives claim this is taking over the leadership and therefore resist aggressiveness in sex. But the same wives may be very aggressive in other areas without any problem. For example, it doesn't bother them to prepare meals without asking their husband's permission. They don't wait for the husband to tell them to make the beds, change dirty diapers, buy groceries, or clean the house. They initiate these actions out of a desire to be responsible. Since God commands a wife to use her body to satisfy her husband, initiating sex is not removing her husband's leadership but is obedience to God's commands. Obviously He will not contradict Himself and in this passage tell her to do something He has forbidden in other passages. For her to wait on her husband to express his desire for sex, passively offer herself, or simply let him have sex, is a clear violation of this principle. It is her responsibility to be aggressive in satisfying the sexual desires of her husband. To fulfill this biblical principle means that there should be very few times when a husband will ask his wife for satisfaction of sexual desires. She must use the list received from her husband to guide her as she initiates satisfying him sexually. When she has completely satisfied him, she knows that she has rightly used her body.

When one wife understood this she got a look of horror on her face. She said that if she focused on satisfying her husband that way, "We'd never get out of bed." Her counselor assured her that her husband wasn't the man she feared. At first, until his desire was satisfied, intercourse would be more frequent. But as she satisfied his desire, the frequency would slow down. Very few men can keep up the pace their wives fear. She can actually bring him to the point where he is begging her to stop. He has to have an erection, whereas all she needs is plenty of lubrication.

To repeat, a wife who is not aggressive in sex is guilty of sinful selfishness. It is irresponsible for her to wait for her husband to ask her to assume each of her home responsibilities. It is just as irresponsible and sinful for her to wait for him to express his sexual desire. He should be so satisfied by her that he doesn't need to ask for sex. When a wife refuses to do this because of lack of interest, she is using her body to satisfy herself by having no sex and is violating the use of the authority or control of her body.

On the other hand, the husband must be more enthusiastic about satisfying his wife than he is in having her satisfy him. Although the problem of failing to initiate sexual activity seems to occur more frequently in wives, all that is said to the wife here must be said equally forcefully to the husband. His focus is to be on satisfying his wife, not demanding that she satisfy him. He is to initiate sexual activity for the purpose of satisfying her, not himself. He has properly used his body when he has used it to provide sexual satisfaction for his wife.

Each partner should so focus on satisfying the other that a lack of satisfaction would rarely be found in either spouse. If a husband seeks sexual pleasure outside the marriage this is heinous, blatantly selfish sin. Was his wife fulfilling her responsibility to provide complete sexual satisfaction for him? He has no excuse for his sin, but if she wasn't she has contributed to his sin by her failure and is accountable to God for that. More will be said on this in the last two principles.

There are also some problems to be addressed concerning this principle. A couple states, "We have different levels of desire." There is nothing in Scripture to deny that those differences are the result of learning and circumstances, or essentially cultural training. Based on much reading and study, I am convinced that these different levels of desire brought into the marriage are learned. They were not developed by God and they were not created in the individual, but they were learned through the society in which one was brought up, and they can be changed through biblical retraining.

Someone might ask, "But what if they're not learned? What if some day you find out you're wrong and we were created with different levels of desire?" That's a good question, but the issue is not different levels of desire but God's guidelines in the sexual relationship. Since the biblical goal of the sexual relationship is giving pleasure, the motivation is not from the level of personal desire but on pleasing God by pleasing one's spouse. God's Word teaches you to do what is necessary to sexually satisfy your mate instead of focusing on your level of desire.

To say one person is oversexed or the other is undersexed is not true if you believe in the Sovereignty of God. It is declaring that God allowed two people to marry who could not obey biblical principles. Such terms say God made a mistake and gave you a mate who cannot satisfy you. Hiding behind such terms, and using them as an excuse to refuse to use your body to satisfy your mate is rebellion against God. It says that I Corinthians 10:13 is invalid. To use such an excuse is to functionally declare, "I will not obey God since I don't like what is happening to me in the process. I'm not getting the sexual satisfaction I want so I will not obey. God doesn't know what it takes to satisfy me and since I know better than He, I'll function on my own." This grieves God and certainly leads to more grief and sorrow for the one who rebels because "the way of the transgressor is hard" (Proverbs 13:15). The problem is not how you were created but your willingness to obey God and to seek to please Him by pleasing your spouse.

From all of this it can be seen that the sexual relationship is to be equal and reciprocal. There is to be mutual initiation of stimulation, foreplay, intercourse, and participation in the sexual act. Marital rights in the sexual relationship "involve also the obligation of mutual responsibility."[1] God has given husband and wife bodies that are to be used to satisfy each other. He gave them the ability that is adequate for the needs and desires of the other person. The Word of God does encourage open and honest communication about those desires. A couple focusing on biblical love and sex can honestly communicate what each enjoys in the sexual relationship and know that pressure will not be applied to get those desires satisfied. Demanding sexual satisfaction is forbidden but requesting it is not. When the principles of 1 Corinthians 7:3–4 are followed, requests will occur infrequently.

To summarize: the primary goal of the sexual relationship is pleasing your spouse. You were each given a body and equal ability to satisfy each other. You have no authority to use your body for yourself. The greatest pleasure comes from satisfying your spouse, not satisfying yourself. The Bible does not allow demanding satisfaction or being passive in the sexual relationship. The focus is on aggressively satisfying each other so that requests for satisfaction are greatly reduced.

---

1. Adams, J. E., *The Christian Counselor's Manual*, Presbyterian & Reformed, 1973, p. 392.

5

Encouraging Pleasure

Pleasure in sex is not sinful and forbidden but rather is assured and encouraged; Proverbs 5:18–19.

> Let your fountain be blessed, and rejoice with the wife of your youth. As a loving deer and a graceful doe, let her breasts satisfy you at all times; and always be enraptured with her love (NKJV).

Proverbs is a delightful book. In the first seven chapters Solomon repeatedly emphasizes to his son the wiles and danger of adulterous relationships. In chapter 5 he gives a contrast between a relationship with the adulterous person and the proper kind of sexual relationship in marriage. In verses 18 and 19 he describes the delights of a marital sexual relationship. Verse 18 clearly focuses and limits the relationship to marriage by the use of the word "wife." Then he repeats the fact that the relationship is with the wife by using the pronoun "her" in verse 19. The word "wife" here is a literal wife but it can be generically used to apply to either mate: the principle he teaches the husband also applies to the wife. He is saying that the most delightful sexual satisfaction will come only from one's mate. All attempts to find it outside marriage will be unsuccessful. Restricting sex to marriage provides the greatest delights in sex. The writer eliminates anybody else, not only in one's actions, but also in his thoughts.

This is taught by other biblical passages:

> I will set nothing wicked before my eyes.
> (Psalm 101:3a, NKJV)

> I have made a covenant with my eyes; why then should I look upon a young woman?
> (Job 31:1, NKJV)

Job wouldn't even look at or think about the sexual features of any woman other than his wife. Also in Matthew 5:28 Jesus warns about the kind of thoughts a person can have and how wrong they are:

> But I say to you that whoever looks at a woman
> to lust for her has already committed adultery
> with her in his heart (NKJV).

He is warning against the wrong kind of look, which leads to lust, which is sin. The man who looks at women's bodies with the excuse that God wants us to appreciate beautiful things is childish. He is using sin-cursed thinking to excuse behavior not condoned in the Bible. He is also saying the physical body of a woman is the only thing about her that is beautiful. God's work in her life is certainly ignored in such juvenile statements. Men need to learn to look only at a woman's face if she is not his wife. God's plan is for a man to receive sexual stimulation from only one source, his wife. This principle does not change for a single man. Since he has no wife he needs to work to prevent sexual stimulation from any source. Also, women need to dress in such a way so as not to draw a man's attention away from her face to her body.

Real sexual delight is thus to be reserved for marriage. The book *Intended For Pleasure* has a great title. God did intend sexual activity for pleasure but the intense delight of that pleasure can only be found in marriage as the rest of Proverbs 5:19 teaches.

The first consideration in these verses is for one to delight in the person of his spouse. The words "loving deer and graceful doe" picture her pleasantness. These are graceful, beautiful, pleasant animals that are enjoyable to have around. My wife and I live in a clearing in the woods. We have a salt block at the edge of the woods, and our geothermal heat pump is continually emptying fresh water into a nearby ravine, which leads to a nearby stream. Deer are drawn to these and will even come near the house and eat birdseed from the ground beneath the bird feeders. Thus we frequently see deer in our yard and enjoy watching these delicate, graceful, beautiful animals. They are of such a nature, one wishes it were possible to develop a relationship that would allow petting.

With this description Solomon portrays the pleasantness of a wife. He's speaking about the desire for her as a companion, as a person. He is commanding development of a deep, intimate relationship on levels other than the physical. Is there a delight in being with her just as a human being, as a person? Is there as much delight in her person as there is in her sexuality? He is saying there should be, if she is being treated as she should be. He is telling the husband, "You are to have a greater desire for her companionship as a person than as a sexual partner. She is your *best* friend, your best buddy." Of all the people in the world, with whom do you most want to be? He's teaching that if your best friend is not your spouse, you haven't developed the kind of biblical companionship God wants you to have. God wants you to delight in being with your spouse. Your greatest delight should be when you spend time with your mate rather than with any other human. Although he is addressing the husband, the principle also applies to the wife.

It is easy to overlook how failure to apply this principle may make it easy for the wife to go outside of marriage. She meets a man who is kind to her and pays attention to her. He listens to her. He compliments her. She finds in the initial relationship with him some desired elements that are lacking in her relationship with her husband. As they continue discussions, she shares some of her marital problems and gains the sympathy of the other man. For the first time in a long time she enjoys the time with a pleasant man. She is finding the kind of companionship reserved for marriage with a man who is not her husband. She is focusing on her desire rather than pleasing God and becoming more like Christ in a marriage where her husband doesn't provide all that she would like. Her satisfaction with some other man is actually criticism of God for not giving her that kind of husband. With this kind of thinking and motivation, she has set aside God's principles and may easily slide into an adulterous relationship. This is why, here in Proverbs, God teaches that *companionship* in marriage is key to the delights of the sexual relationship.

Delight in companionship leads to delight in the sexual relationship. The word "breasts" is not an allegorical term referring to some spiritual relationship. The whole context refers to the sexual relationship; thus the word signifies specific sexual organs. Her sexuality is also a source of delight and satisfaction. He is saying that her breasts, referring to her physical body – her sexuality – are to be a source of satisfaction at all times.

The word "satisfy" pictures a person in a dry desert; he's very thirsty and his mouth is so parched he can hardly talk; it feels like the walls of his mouth are beginning to draw in on one another because of such intense dryness. Then he is given a cool drink of water that is of such quantity that he continues to drink until his thirst is satisfied completely. The water is cool, refreshing, delightful, pleasant, and extremely satisfying. His thirst is completely satisfied. The sexual relationship is to be as refreshing, delightful and satisfying as that drink of water. To repeat an earlier statement, the wife should not just passively offer her body, or be willing to have sex, but aggressively use her body to bring complete satisfaction to her husband. Since this applies to marriage, it applies to either spouse. The husband is to focus on providing a delightfully satisfying sexual relationship for his wife; he is to satisfy her by her standards, not his. This is not something the wife offers and the husband receives but something each initiates in giving.

Not only should the sexual relationship satisfy like quenching the thirst but the verse goes even further. The word "enraptured" (NKJV) or "exhilarated" (NASB) is translated "ravished" in the KJV. It literally means *to be drunk or intoxicated*. This is the only place in the Bible where intoxication is approved and encouraged. He is to be intoxicated by, overwhelmed with, completely satisfied by this relationship.

It might be compared to the satisfaction one has at the end of a delicious buffet meal. You eat and eat and eat and eat and then say, "I can't eat another bite." Someone brings another piece of your favorite pie, but it doesn't even *look* good. You have been so delightfully overwhelmed or intoxicated by the meal that more food is not interesting. The word "ravished" implies such complete satisfaction that there is *no desire for more*. When your mate is so satisfied that there is no more interest, he has no need to look for satisfaction elsewhere. In fact, if temptation does come there is little response because you have already most delightfully satisfied him.

What Solomon says to the husband in these verses enhances what Paul teaches in 1 Corinthians 7, verses 3 and 4. Each is to provide this kind of delightful sexual satisfaction for his spouse, to make certain his spouse is intoxicated or overwhelmed with satisfaction. The husband is not to focus on satisfying himself, but he should find such great delight in satisfying his wife that she is satisfied and overwhelmed with satisfaction. The wife is not to offer sex to her husband as a dutiful drudgery, but delightfully provide the satisfying, pleasant relationship described. Even though the sexual relationship is a duty and a responsibility, it is to be an intensely pleasant duty. The end result will be that neither one can be attracted by someone outside the marriage. You can measure, to some degree, when you have followed 1 Corinthians 7, verses 3 and 4, by your spouse's being so satiated it would be difficult to be tempted into a sexual relationship outside of marriage.

How can this be done? Here is a list of some things that will help increase each other's delight:

1. The most important factor is to have the right goal in the sexual relationship. This means to focus on giving sexual satisfaction to each other and to recognize that biblical sex is delightful. The primary goal is giving, not getting, pleasure.

2. Solve problems. Unconfessed sin hinders the focus on giving. Many times the sexual relationship is seen through the failures of the other. With this kind of focus, the sexual relationship may be used as a punishment or reward for the other's failures or good deeds. In counseling, I do not recall seeing any sexual problems that did not have unresolved conflicts involved in some way.

3. Avoid distractions. Put out of the mind the things that interfere.

4. Provide for the right kind of atmosphere. Doors should have locks on them so a husband and wife can have privacy. When children are present, they should be taught that they cannot enter the parent's bedroom without permission. Both husband and wife need to teach the children respect for your closed door. There is no problem with parents asking children to go do something while they retire to the bedroom for some private time even in the middle of the day, and no need to explain to the children what they are doing. There must be freedom to be completely uninhibited within their room without the fear of being heard or someone entering the room unexpectedly.

5. The husband must be very patient with his wife. Some husbands are only concerned about satisfying themselves and become impatient. It is very important for a husband to be very gentle. Real godly manliness is characterized by gentleness, not roughness. On occasions the wife also may be in a hurry to get it over with, as a duty to be tolerated, with as little involvement as possible.

6. Allow adequate time for foreplay. Couples need to take time to stimulate each other. Foreplay is part of the biblical process of satisfying each other. It is a part of God's plan for the sexual relationship. It fits the biblical view of giving. Do the things that are pleasant to each other for

the purpose of pleasing God. The act of pleasing each other communicates love.

7. Make sure each has a clean body and breath and the husband is shaved as well (if he shaves). Bad breath and body odor do not make it pleasant to be near a person. Every couple needs a sex kit – soap, washcloth, towel, tooth brush, tooth paste, razor, aftershave lotion, perfume and lubrication. The proper use of aftershave lotions, perfumes, and colognes are useful. "Bathing and shaving at night will show love, respect, and an anticipation of closeness."[1]

8. Have adequate lubrication for the wife. Water-soluble lubrication like KY jelly is available at any drug store. When this is not present she will very likely experience considerable discomfort, even to the point of pain.

9. Be spontaneous. Sexual activity need not be confined to a dark bedroom. Make plans for other non-structured times.

10. Communicate about the things that increase pleasure. Reading some good books together may help (such as the one mentioned above,[2] the Song of Solomon, etc.).

Real sex, as God designed it, is found only within marriage. One may find pleasure in sexual relationships outside of marriage, but this cannot be the real, intimate, deep type of relationship that God has designed. Only when one follows biblical principles within the marriage can God's plans for the human experience be achieved. In past decades there was a fear that people would not have a good sexual relationship until they discovered their sexual compatibility prior to marriage. Such ideas never achieve their goals. A man cannot achieve this kind of satisfaction by violating biblical princi-

1. E. Wheat, G. Wheat, *Intended For Pleasure*, Revell, Grand Rapids, 1977, Rev. 1987, p. 81
2. Ibid.

ples, because he was created by God to find satisfaction only by pleasing God. Pleasure that is sought as the source of satisfaction is transient, elusive, and actually *not* satisfying. Of course, marriage does not guarantee that sex will be delightful, but the key is that sexual delight is actually a by-product of obedience to God.

6

The Pattern of Sex

Sexual relations are to be regular and continuous;
1 Corinthians 7:5.

We left 1 Corinthians 7 for a brief excursion into Proverbs 5 to point out that the duties in the sexual relationship should not be drudgery but very delightful.

Returning to 1 Corinthians 7, we read in verse 5:

> Do not deprive one another except with consent for a time, that you may give yourselves to fasting and prayer; and come together again so that Satan does not tempt you because of your lack of self-control (NKJV).

> Don't deprive one another, except by agreement for a time that you may devote yourselves to prayer. Then come together again so that Satan may not be able to tempt you because of your lack of self-control (CCNT).

The word "deprive" (or "defraud" in KJV) means to withhold or avoid through deceit or dishonesty. It is withholding sex from each other for selfish, dishonest reasons. These excuses may include such things as saying one is "too tired," or "has a headache," or "has a big day tomorrow," or "is busy reading the newspaper or watching television," simply to avoid sex. A wife may *say* she has a headache and does not want sex, but actually she is mad at her husband. One husband, at bedtime, took his wife a glass of water and two aspirin to which she asked, "What is that for?" He graciously replied, "Your headache." To which she responded in surprise, "But I don't have a headache!" With a big grin on his face her husband exclaimed, "Gotcha."

Avoiding sex can become a way of getting back at him for something he did or didn't do. It is her way to pay him back for some hurt. Personal desires have become more important than meeting the desires of the spouse. This is using sex as a tool to punish, bargain, or reward. It's using sex manipulatively.

Of course a wife may honestly tell her husband that she is very tired or that there is a real physical problem. For example, suppose a husband expresses to his wife his desire for sex. She is quite tired and has a big day tomorrow, resulting in a diminished desire for the sexual relationship. What should she do? She should be honest and describe these things in honest communication that pleases God, not manipulate her husband. However, she should still be willing to go ahead to please God by pleasing her husband. When he hears these things, a loving biblical husband should immediately change his focus from sexual desire to providing love, understanding, and encouragement for his wife. He must focus on *her* desires, not *his*; he should thank her for being honest with him, express his love for her, and be willing to honor her desires by not having sex. This may seem to some like an impasse: the wife is willing to go ahead and the husband is willing not to go ahead. So what should they do? In the situation just described, they should not have sex. The husband has stated his preference but the wife has stated some factors that are far more critical than preference and that make it difficult for her to participate in sex. She has been honest and her husband should recognize and honor her honesty. She should recognize his love and his willingness to change for her benefit and gratefully receive his love and consideration of her desires. If he is unloving and insists on going ahead, she should focus on satisfying him, not trying to avoid sex to get what she wants.

Abstinence must be by mutual consent (1 Corinthians 7:5). In other words, *both* must agree to abstain from sexual activity. One cannot refuse the other nor withhold sex because his mate is upset or wants to punish him. Nor is sex to be used as a reward for good behavior or for doing nice things. Observing this factor prevents the sinful use of sex as a weapon or bargaining agent.

The question is not, "Shall we have sex?" or, "When shall we have sex?" or, "When are you going to want sex?" or even, "When are you going to let me have sex?" but, "When shall we *not* have sex?" The mutual consent in this verse is not when to *have* sex but when both mutually consent to *refrain* from sex. This fulfills the biblical command to satisfy each other sexually. Paul is not teaching 24-hour-a-day sex, or a sexual marathon, but focuses on keeping the spouse satiated. Sexual activity is to be thought of from this perspective.

In this verse there are four guidelines for refraining. The first one, already stated, is by mutual consent. Both agree; one does not withhold sex as a bargaining chip or punishment weapon. The second guideline is that refraining is for a specific period of time that both have predetermined and prearranged. It is not to be carried on indefinitely. The third guideline is that there is a specific goal in mind when sex is avoided. The scripture refers to prayer[1] but this is not a limiting phrase. Even though the passage only mentions prayer, the various commentaries on this verse do not make prayer the only reason to limit the activity. A husband and wife may refrain from sex because of surgery, such as hysterectomy, for a trip one or both must make, or for other mutually acceptable reasons. They both voluntarily agree to avoid sexual activity for a specific period of time for a specific godly goal upon which they have both agreed. The fourth guideline is that abstinence is terminated by reestablishing the sexual relationship. Both can anticipate such an event since they both have predetermined when it will occur. Many sexual conflicts would be solved if husband and wife were honest and used this biblical principle in their relationship. This does not remove the principle of moderation and consideration for the

---

1. "And fasting" in older translations.

other. Consideration for each other regulates requests and refusals. It does not demand satisfaction.

People often ask how frequently a couple should participate in the sexual relationship. These verses in 1 Corinthians answer the question under two guidelines. The first guideline is that it should be often enough to keep each other satisfied to enhance self-control. From verse 9 we see that there should be no burning, unfulfilled desire. Each needs to understand the other's definition of satisfaction through good communication. Many a person has lost their spouse because, for sinful reasons, sexual satisfaction was not provided in the marriage. Most of the requests for unusual sexual activity or for activities that one or the other may find offensive come from unsatisfied sexual desire. Passionate sex many times will prevent these desires and demands or at least stop them. Consideration for the spouse regulates frequency. When a husband is making requests for varieties of sexual activity not pleasing to his wife, she can significantly reduce those requests and possibly remove them, by aggressively providing frequent pleasant sex in other ways. When she does this, she should make it her goal to have so much sex, he literally requests that she stop. And he will ask her to stop because he must have an erection every time, which cannot simply be produced by an act of the will (like the movement of an extremity).

The other guideline for frequency is also in the same verse. It is to be frequent enough to avoid temptation. Satan's temptations are continuous. He uses unsatisfied desire to tempt to sin. James also points out that we are tempted by our own desires (James 1:14). Verse 9 also teaches that the sexual relationship in marriage is what solves the problem of unsatisfied, unfulfilled desire. When a partner withholds sex for unbiblical reasons, this may produce unsatisfied desire and may give Satan an opportunity to tempt through lack of self-control. Unnecessary abstinence makes self-control more difficult. Satan's continuous efforts to tempt to sexual sin become more difficult to resist. This doesn't excuse sin even though it makes it easier to sin. Sexual desire should be satisfied so continuously that there is no desire for unusual or unbiblical sexual activity. The goal of giving pleasure in sex is to provide such complete sexual satisfaction that Satan cannot tempt the individual. This does not remove the principle of moderation or consideration for each other. Nor does it excuse unreasonable demands. Biblical love expressed in showing consideration for the other will regulate requests and refusals.

Conclusion

We have looked at six principles from the Bible.

1. *Sex in marriage is pure and holy.*

2. *Sex is not the basis of marriage, and marriage is not first and foremost a physical union.*

3. *The goal of the sexual relationship is to provide sexual satisfaction for one's spouse.*

4. *Both have equal ability to satisfy each other.*

5. *Pleasure in sex is not forbidden, but assumed and encouraged.*

6. *Sexual relations are to be regular and continuous.*

These six principles, along with the biblical view of marriage, provide the basic structure a couple needs for good sexual relationships in marriage. These principles should be taught to children, not just pertaining to sexual relationships but as a part of the whole view of marriage. These principles should be taught in premarital counseling so that a couple enters a marriage with these views. Couples planning marriage do not need extensive knowledge of sexual functions prior to marriage. Starting with these principles, a time set aside to learn about sex with a good book is one important function of the honeymoon. A book I recommend is *Intended for Pleasure.*[1]

If a couple is having sexual difficulty or conflict in the sexual relationship, it would be good for them to learn these

---

1. E. Wheat, G. Wheat, *Intended For Pleasure*, Revell, Grand Rapids, 1977, Rev. 1987. *The Journal of Pastoral Practice*, Volume 3, Number 4, has a review of the first edition of the book. Some needed cautions are also found in that review.

six principles. It would be wise at the conclusion of the study of each principle for each spouse to evaluate his own personal attitude toward that principle. The couple should discuss their own personal attitudes, followed by a discussion of the attitude one observes in the other. When they find that their own personal attitudes and actions differ from biblical principles, they should work together to make them consistent with God's Word. When they learn defects about themselves and see defects in each other, they should not feel threatened; they should consider each other as teammates striving to be the kind of couple that pleases God. Changes they need to make should be spelled out in terms of specific actions.

When Christian couples practice biblical sex, they will proclaim the Gospel as it is seen in the marriage relationship. Their companionship should grow and develop in all areas of their relationship, including the sexual area. Sex must fit the overall picture of marriage relationships. Two people must grow in all their relationships with each other. They must have deep intimacy and interpenetration in every area of their life – spiritually, mentally, and physically. As they discuss other areas of life, it will be easier to discuss the sexual relationship. These principles should be memorized and made a very vital part of their lives.

People who are so vitally involved in the lives of others must stay vitally involved with their own spouse. They must build deep companionship and relationship with each other. Being committed to Christ, each other, and biblical principles will make the total marriage relationship a living picture of Christ's relationship to His bride.

The word "sex" needs to be rescued from the world's misuse. Remember, the world's view focuses on receiving pleasure. Even though God designed sex as very pleasant, receiving pleasure is not His goal. Pleasure is to be received as a by-product of sex. In the biblical view, pleasure comes from giving, not receiving. The goal of sex is not personal climax, but pleasing one's spouse. Sexual activity is to be motivated by the desire to give pleasure to and satisfy one's spouse.

These concepts need to be lived out and taught in homes and churches. The world needs to see what sex ought to be.

In conclusion, God has designed the sexual relationship so that the really delightful aspects which can only be found in marriage are more than simply the physical sensations. Only when you follow biblical principles within marriage can God's plans for the human experience be achieved. The result of this will be a sexual relationship that is deeply satisfying and glorifying to God.